happiness is …

happiness is ...

200 celebrations of sisterhood

Lisa Swerling & Ralph Lazar

CHRONICLE BOOKS

SAN FRANCISCO

a tub of ice cream
and two spoons

good old-fashioned fun

a friend in any
weather

doing anything and everything
together

treat time!

sharing cool
stuff with you
online

feeling anything is possible
with you by my side

sharing trashy magazines

an unbreakable bond

random acts of
weirdness

having you on speed
dial in case of an
emergency

scaring ourselves

a friend for
life

Thelma & Louise

making up after an argument

surprising you

thinking alike

letting you have
the bigger half

always being
pleased to see you

seeing eye to eye

reading something
you recommended

dancing like nobody's
watching

letting you take the helm

knowing we have each
other's backs

a joint effort

waking up in a
beautiful place

staying connected

endless chats

being in it
together

letting guys be part of the sisterhood,
occasionally

hosting the best
parties

having someone
to rely on

getting you the
perfect gift

your awesome moves

the excitement of
seeing you after
time apart

a shared experience

helping you reorganize

a real letter
from you

new sisterhoods in the making

knowing you're
there for me when
it really counts

walking down your street

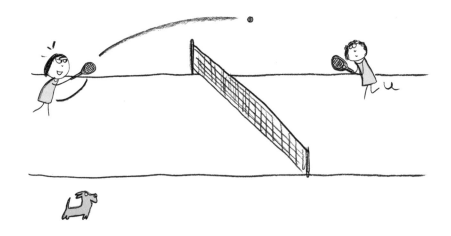

healthy competition

the funny things you say

buying something you'll love

someone who
knows me better
than anyone

a weekend full of great plans

annual rituals

finding you
the perfect
greeting card

F.R.I.E.N.D.S.

starting a long-
term project

leading the pack

watching your
confidence grow

having the same
obsessions

showing up in matching outfits

laughing till our
faces hurt

staying up
all night

planning a big
event together

being your plus one

big get-togethers

shared
interests

being in unison

the best vacations

when your closet
is my closet

the start of a big
adventure

being unapologetically sappy

a slumber party

having you by my side

feeling understood

being happy when
you're happy

quietly appeciating
your amazingness

a sister who is a
best friend

when you're the
star of the show

endless days
of summer

dancing in the new year

a hug sandwich

warmth and harmony

a spontaneous
meal together

quiet time

simple coexistence

an awesome threesome

traveling long distances
just to see you

getting messy

a full life, experienced
together

having someone I can
talk to about anything

singing through traffic jams

being dumber
than dumb
and dumber

a long walk with no time pressure

making each other LOL

staying up late

living the good life

free therapy

sharing life's milestones

planning a
trip together

living in the same
neighborhood

having deep
discussions

crazy shenanigans

spa nights at home

seeing your name pop up on my phone

sisterhood across
generations

trying new
things

exercise as an excuse
to catch up

knowing what
you like

Carrie, Charlotte, Samantha & Miranda

sharing secrets

a heart-to-heart connection

an indulgent
weekend away

seeing your talents shine

a shoulder
to cry on

helping you
unpack

having you
in my life

binge-watching TV at
the end of a long week

a girls' night out

getting the
giggles

feeling close even when
we're far apart

an epic road trip

being together for
the big moments

a comfortable silence

tears of joy

staying in touch no
matter what

having a conversation
with just one look

clothing
swaps

exploring the world together

camping in the backyard

a joint enterprise

running into you
unexpectedly

cheering you on

a gossip
session

 wearing the same
shade of lipstick

calling you first when
I have good news

 being understood

singing along to the radio

telling you every detail
of my night out

making our own rules

knowing that I totally,
totally, totally love you

when mi casa
es tu casa

sending you my
first drafts

being enlightened

Venus & Serena

growing up together

cooking something up

sharing the things you
can only tell a sister

being the loudest ones
at the party

sharing

a workout buddy

friends who become sisters

taking a class together

a long awaited
video chat

a double
date

a song that reminds
me of you

getting
dolled up

togetherness

being chill

when we're the
only ones laughing

helping you achieve your
dreams

a warm hug

being an aunt to your children

our silly selves

rocking out

knowing what
you're thinking

celebrating
success

a pinky promise
that we'll never
break

teamwork

goofy selfies

trying out the latest crazes

never-ending group texts

playing around in the park

fancy cocktails for
no particular reason

a choreographed
dance routine

playing a duet

feeling sophisticated and grown-up

the perfect picnic

joining together to
change the world

a "say cheese"
moment

holding hands
just because

sharing strong opinions

seeing amazing things
with you

a reunion

conversations that
never end

going through old photos

best friends forever

getting crafty

being joined
at the hip

childhood
friendships

making memories

jokes no one else
would understand

never running out
of things to say

staying friends for years
and years

a circle of strong
women

Jo, Amy, Beth
and Meg March

seeing who finishes
their lollipop last

in-jokes only we
understand

a very civilized
sleepover

a movie
marathon

Elsa & Anna

when you spoil me

being together on
birthdays

the earliest shared memories

a connection that gets
stronger every year

a gaggle of girls!

ISBN 978-1-4521-4271-5
Manufactured in China.

Design by Lisa Swerling and Ralph Lazar

10 9 8 7 6 5 4 3 2 1

Chronicle Books LLC
680 Second Street
San Francisco, California 94107
www.chroniclebooks.com